PLAY and LEARN

1 year old

63 simple activities

Learn while having fun

Quality time for parents and children

The activities in this book are organized into the following sections:

Special thanks to Joan Henry and Jean Tuemmler, my Mulberry Tree teaching team.

Congratulations on your purchase of some of the finest teaching materials in the world.

For information about other Evan-Moor products, call 1-800-777-4362 or FAX 1-800-777-4332

Visit our website http://www.evan-moor.com. Check the Product Updates link for supplements, additions, and corrections for this book.

Author:	Jill Norris
Editor:	Marilyn Evans
Copy Editor:	Cathy Harber
Illustrator:	Cindy Davis
Designer:	Cheryl Puckett
Desktop:	Carolina Caird
Cover:	Cheryl Puckett

Entire contents ©1999 by EVAN-MOOR CORP.
18 Lower Ragsdale Drive, Monterey, CA 93940-5746.
Permission is hereby granted to the individual purchaser to reproduce student materials in this book for noncommercial individual or classroom use only. Permission is not granted for schoolwide, or systemwide, reproduction of materials.
Printed in U.S.A.

EMC 4503

How to Play and Learn with Your Four-Year-Old

What can I do to help my four-year-old learn and have fun at the same time? This book answers that question with 63 simple activities that parents can do as they spend quality time with their four-year-olds. Each activity is fun and provides a positive learning experience.

Play and learn at bath time or when you're waiting in line. Have activities ready if you're riding in the car and when your child is getting ready for bed. Sitting at the table, playing outside, or sharing a story—wherever you are and whatever you're doing—you can provide the kinds of experiences that build the foundation for future learning.

Use this book as a resource. Read over the activities to become familiar with them, but don't worry about doing them precisely. Enjoy the special time you spend with your child and remember:

• **Many four-year-olds love to have a choice.**
>   Have two or three activities ready and let your child choose one.

• **Your four-year-olds may love to repeat things.**
>   Do the activities often.

• **Four-year-olds love to make up their own games.**
>   Make up new activities using those in the book as a pattern.

Most of your child's learning comes from play.
During play your child:
>   • gains a sense of competency and control.
>   • learns about how people and things work.
>   • makes connections between concrete things and abstract ideas.

Building Blocks to Learning

Variety is important.

Playing and learning should be like sampling a relaxed smorgasbord. As a parent you provide the balanced menu. Your child is responsible for making the selection. Tempt your child with exciting possibilities and spark his or her interest in new areas, but don't force-feed activities that you choose.

Activities should be hands-on.

You want to help your child think. Listening uses only a small part of the brain. Looking or watching uses a bit more, while writing uses still more. Experiences where thinking, feeling, and moving happen together require your child to use many parts of the brain at the same time. These multilevel activities are especially important for young learners.

Encourage spontaneity.

Rules should be kept to a minimum. Make consistent rules regarding safety and respect for others. Provide plenty of room for movement. Have fun and enjoy learning.

Skills for Success

Each page in *Play and Learn* is labeled to tell which skill areas are developed by the activity. Often a single activity addresses several different skills. You help to build the foundation for your child's success in school when you provide practice in these six important skills:

 Large-Motor Development
walking, running, jumping, large-muscle movement

 Coordination and Dexterity
small-muscle movements in the hands and fingers

 Language Development
speaking, listening, and developing vocabulary

 Creativity
imagining, exploring different materials, thinking in new ways

 Problem Solving
finding alternative solutions, understanding cause and effect

 Memory and Concentration
remembering, connecting different ideas

Art Time

Red, yellow, blue—
This is fun to do.
Green, purple, pink—
Tell me what you think.

I'm an artist.
Look at me.
I'm an artist.
Don't you agree?

Play and Learn to

- foster creativity
- learn about the properties and qualities of materials
- build sense of independence
- develop imagination
- sharpen perceptions
- improve small- and large-motor coordination

Activities

Sandpaper Rubbings

Creating a rubbing is just like magic!

What You Need

- shapes cut from posterboard or sandpaper
- paper
- crayons

What You Do

1. Put several shapes on a solid surface.

2. Lay the paper on top of the shapes.

3. Rub crayons back and forth across the paper until outlines of the shapes appear.

Vary the activity by:

- using different shapes
- using leaves and pieces of bark
- cutting out sandpaper letters to spell your child's name and hiding them under the paper

My Macaroni Necklace

String macaroni on a shoestring to make a nifty necklace.

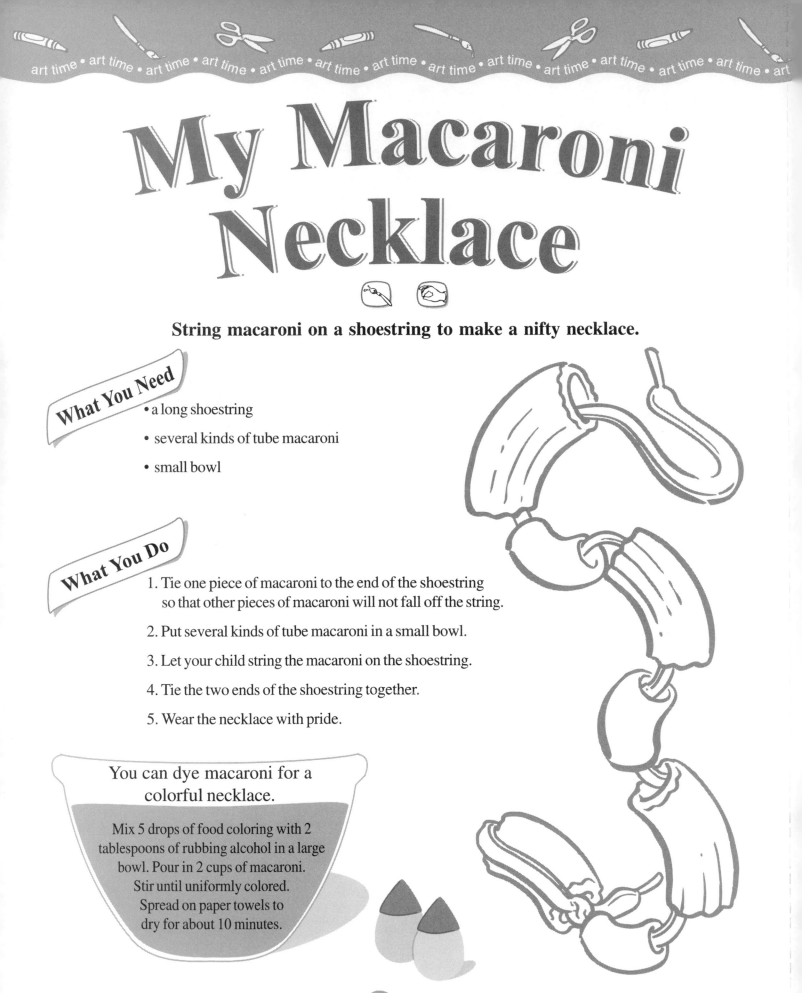

What You Need

- a long shoestring
- several kinds of tube macaroni
- small bowl

What You Do

1. Tie one piece of macaroni to the end of the shoestring so that other pieces of macaroni will not fall off the string.

2. Put several kinds of tube macaroni in a small bowl.

3. Let your child string the macaroni on the shoestring.

4. Tie the two ends of the shoestring together.

5. Wear the necklace with pride.

You can dye macaroni for a colorful necklace.

Mix 5 drops of food coloring with 2 tablespoons of rubbing alcohol in a large bowl. Pour in 2 cups of macaroni. Stir until uniformly colored. Spread on paper towels to dry for about 10 minutes.

Cut & Paste

Cut small pieces of colored paper and glue them onto a background.

Note: Four-year-olds should practice simply cutting before they are expected to cut out specific shapes.

What You Need

• small pieces of colored paper (wrapping paper, Sunday funnies, magazine pages, almost any paper that cuts easily)

• child scissors (Try the scissors to make sure that they cut before you buy them. If your child is left-handed, try them left-handed.)

• larger piece of construction paper

• glue stick

What You Do

1. Have your child cut the colored papers into pieces.

2. Pile the colored pieces into piles.

3. Paste the colored pieces to the large piece of construction paper.

GLUE STIK

Show your child how to hold the scissors with the thumb on top and the pointer finger underneath. Hold your child's hand gently at first to help keep the scissors' blades perpendicular to the paper.

Mount or frame the finished collage and display it on your refrigerator gallery.

Mixing Colors

Mix colored water to make new colors.

What You Need

- an area where spills can occur: kitchen table, linoleum floor, front porch

- small clear plastic cups

- food coloring

- a small plastic pitcher of water (Fill the pitcher only as full as your child can handle easily.)

- towels for clean-up

- stick for stirring

What You Do

1. Set out three small plastic cups.

2. Put three drops of food coloring in each cup.

3. Have your child pour a little water into each cup.

4. Talk about the colors you see.

5. Set out another cup.

6. Have your child pour a little water from two of the colored-water cups into the empty cup.

7. Ask your child to tell you about what happened.

8. Have your child try more combinations. Encourage free exploration!

Dip skinny strips of paper towel into the cups of colored water.

Paste the strips on another piece of paper for a pretty paper collage.

Pudding Painting

Finger paint with pudding.

What You Need

- a place to work where spills won't cause disaster
- two plastic trays
- water for clean-up
- a sponge for clean-up
- enough pudding to cover the bottom of the trays

What You Do

1. Wash your hands.

2. Cover the bottom of a clean plastic tray with a thin layer of pudding.

3. Draw a picture with your finger.

4. Try moving your fingers and hand in different ways to create different effects. Show your child some of these different ways of painting:

tip of finger	finger flat	side of finger
fingers together	palm of hand	side of hand

5. Smooth the pudding with your hand and start over as many times as you like.

Spoon leftover pudding into cups for a postpainting party and enjoy licking your fingers.

Finger Paint Masterpiece

Create a colorful painting with finger paint.

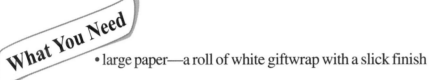

What You Need

- large paper—a roll of white giftwrap with a slick finish
- finger paint—purchased or homemade
- plastic tray

What You Do

1. Before you begin, set up a drying area (a plastic tablecloth spread on a table or on a hard-surface floor out of the traffic pattern). Cut the white paper to fit in the tray.

2. Wash your hands.

3. Spoon a scoop of paint onto the paper.

4. Smear and draw with your fingers and hands.

5. Add different colors to the picture.

6. Move the paper to the drying area and repeat with new paper.

Homemade Finger Paint

Mix ½ cup (63 g) of cornstarch and 3 tablespoons (36 g) of sugar. Add 2 cups (36 ml) of water. Stir over low heat until blended. Divide into 4 equal portions. Put each portion in an empty margarine tub or similar container. Add a different food color and several drops of liquid detergent to each portion.

Clay

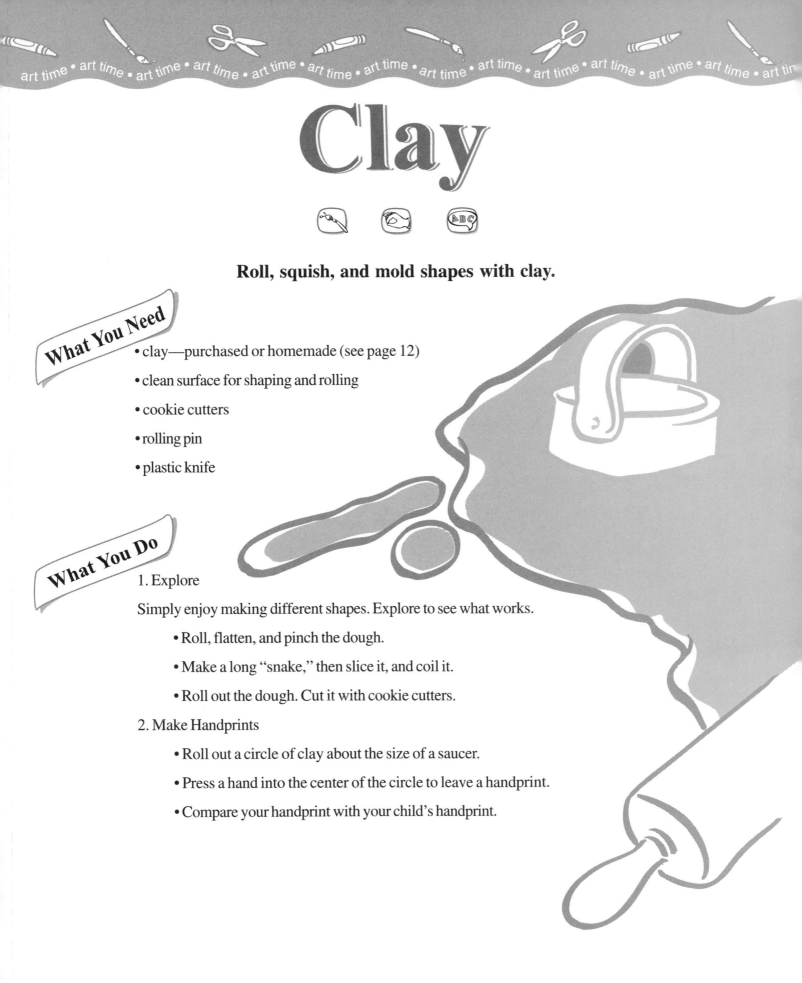

Roll, squish, and mold shapes with clay.

What You Need

- clay—purchased or homemade (see page 12)
- clean surface for shaping and rolling
- cookie cutters
- rolling pin
- plastic knife

What You Do

1. Explore

Simply enjoy making different shapes. Explore to see what works.

- Roll, flatten, and pinch the dough.
- Make a long "snake," then slice it, and coil it.
- Roll out the dough. Cut it with cookie cutters.

2. Make Handprints

- Roll out a circle of clay about the size of a saucer.
- Press a hand into the center of the circle to leave a handprint.
- Compare your handprint with your child's handprint.

Note about ready-made clays:

- Oil-based clays leave oily marks on surfaces and can be difficult to clean up.

- Playdough® is easy to shape and clean up, but it dries out quickly when exposed to the air.

Recipe for Modeling Dough

- 1 cup (125 g) of flour

- ¼ cup (72 g) of salt

- 3-ounce package (85 g) of Jell-O®

- 1 tablespoon (15 ml) of vegetable oil

- 1 cup (240 ml) of water

- 2 tablespoons (16 g) of cream of tartar

Mix all ingredients together. Stir over medium heat for 3 to 5 minutes until dough begins to form. Turn out onto lightly floured surface and knead. Store in an airtight container.

Recipe for Baker's Clay

- 1 cup (288 g) of salt

- 1½ cups (360 ml) of hot water

- 4 cups (500 g) of flour

Dissolve salt in the hot water. Stir in flour. Knead until pliable (at least 5 minutes). Store in an airtight container. Bake in 250° (120° C) oven until hard. Baking time will depend on the size and thickness of the object. When the object is cool, color it with marking pens, spray with clear glaze, and enjoy.

Mealtime

I can stir and I can slice.
I can set a place so nice.
I can measure and I can beat.
But best of all, I can eat!

Play and Learn to

- identify colors

- learn the names of everyday things

- make patterns with familiar things

- identify shapes

- describe an object

- count, measure, and follow directions

Activities

Eating Colors

Recognize colors as you eat.

What You Need

• a plate of colorful, edible food

What You Do

1. Choose a food on the plate and say,
   I see (color). I'm eating (color).

2. Child chooses a food and says,
   I see (color). I'm eating (color).

3. Continue as long as the activity is "fun."

Make a game out of the color identification.

I'm eating red.
Can you guess what it is?
Yes, red strawberries.
YUM!

What Is It? How Is It Used?

Name utensils and serving pieces and show how they are used.

What You Need

- place settings

What You Do

1. Point to one utensil in the place setting at your table.

2. Ask,
   What is it?

3. After your child responds, say,
   Show me how you use it.

4. Practice this identifying game during food preparation to learn about more utensils. (a potato masher, a spatula, a ladel, a colander, a funnel)

It's a Pattern

Set the table together.

What You Need

- plates
- glasses
- silverware
- napkins

What You Do

1. Set one place setting as a model.

2. Have your child duplicate the place setting.

3. Another day, repeat the activity, adding
   something new —
       put a salad fork on the table
       lay a flower on the napkin

As your child becomes proficient at
repeating the pattern, encourage setting
the table without the model.

 Play and Learn with Your Four-Year-Old • EMC 4503

The Shape of Things

Do this classifying activity when you're having lunch or dinner.

What You Need

- dishes
- foods

What You Do

1. Show a plate to your child. Say,
   This is a circle.

2. Have your child find a dish or food that is a circle shape. Ask,
   Can you see a circle on our table?

3. Try a different shape. Say,
   This slice of bread is a square.
   Can you find another square?

Have your child classify all the foods on the plate and then count the different shapes.
   I have three circles, one square,
   and a funny pile of beans.

I Spy...

Your child guesses what you describe.

Note: I Spy is a great game for many times a day! Mealtime is only one time to play!

What You Need

• a focused moment

What You Do

1. Explain this guessing game to your child. Say,
   *I will look around and choose something that
      I can see.*
   I will tell you the shape and color of the thing.
   You will guess what I chose.
   I will give you more clues if you can't guess.

2. Play the game. Say,
   *I spy with my little eye something that is shaped
      like an ear.*
   It is reddish-brown.

3. Switch roles with your child.

Cook with Me!

Prepare a meal together.

What You Need

- small cutting board or work surface
- food ingredients

What You Do

1. Begin by having your child help you do a single step in food preparation.

2. Then assign preparation of one item.

   - Wash the lettuce leaves.
   - Stir the batter.
   - Cut some fruit.
   - Peel a carrot.
   - Slice the cheese.

Monitor your child's use of knives. Start with nonserrated plastic ones.

four recipes your four-year-old will love making

Ants on a Log

- celery logs
- peanut butter
- raisin ants

Fill the logs with
   peanut butter.
Put raisin ants on top.
Eat Up!

Apple Rings

- apple
- cream cheese
- walnuts

Core an apple.
Stuff center with
   cream cheese
   and walnuts.
Slice and eat.

Cracker Stacks

- crackers
- cheese squares
- salami slices

Stack a snack:
   cracker   cheese
   salami   cracker
Pop it in your mouth.

O.J. Sipper

- orange juice
- lemon-lime soda
- vanilla ice cream

Pour orange juice into
   glass 🥛 ½ full.
Pour soda into glass 🥛 ¾ full.
Add a scoop of ice cream. 🥤

Bigger and Smaller

You and your child compare the size of things.

What You Need

• items on the table at mealtime

What You Do

1. Make an observation. Say,

    The glass of milk is bigger than the salt shaker.

2. Ask your child to identify something else that is bigger than the salt shaker.

    My cup is bigger than the salt shaker.

3. Continue…

    My sandwich is bigger than the salt shaker.

4. Switch to smaller…

    My carrot stick is smaller than the salt shaker.
    My olive is smaller than the salt shaker.

Use other comparing words—longer and shorter, thicker and thinner, stronger and weaker, heavier and lighter.

Indoor Playtime

Let's build a bridge,
A tower, a town.
Build it up high
Then knock it down.

Play and Learn to

- practice counting
- match items
- answer questions
- find hidden objects
- take turns, roll dice, count spaces, make choices, win, and lose
- learn about balance
- stack and build with blocks
- use imagination to solve problems
- copy a pattern

Activities

Try Again!

Play this matching game with a basket of real things.

What You Need

- one big basket or bowl

- two small baskets or bowls

- sets of little objects (at least three of each kind) from the toy chest or junk drawer — pencils, erasers, paper clips, pennies, screws, jar lids, action figures, building blocks

- cardboard lids for the small baskets

What You Do

1. Put all the objects in the big basket.

2. Players should close their eyes and choose six objects from the big basket. Objects are put in the players' small baskets.

3. When the choosing is finished, players should check to see if they have any sets of three objects. Any sets should be placed on the table outside of the basket. Then the players cover their small baskets with the cardboard lids.

4. Player 1 looks in his or her basket and asks Player 2 for an object that will make a match.
   Do you have a pink eraser?
   If Player 2 has a match, it is given to Player 1.

5. If Player 2 does not have a match, he or she says,
   Try again.
   Player 1 takes a new object from the big basket.

6. Players alternate turns until one player has an empty basket.

Note: Anytime a player has a set of 3 matching objects, the objects are placed on the table. Any player can add to any set on the table at any time. You and your child may enjoy playing Go Fish! This traditional card game follows the same format.

Let's Have a Hunt!

Hide a set of objects around the house and then find them.

What You Need

- a container

- a number of the same item (pinecones, wrapped candies, feathers, shells...)

Note: It's a good idea to know how many items you have.

What You Do

1. Hide the items in plain sight around your house.

2. Give your child the container and challenge him or her to find the items.

3. Have your child count the items found. Say,
   I hid _____ things. You found _____ things.
   Did you find all the things that I hid?

As you repeat this activity, try these variations:

- Try hiding items in less obvious places.

- Let your child hide the items. You do the finding.

- Hide two kinds of items.

Play and Learn with Your Four-Year-Old • EMC 4503

How Many?

Count all the windows in your home.

What You Need

• the place where you live

What You Do

1. Ask your child to help you find all the windows in your home.

2. Walk from room to room and keep a tally or a chart.

You can also count the doors, the beds, the stair steps, and the sinks...
Add these counts to your chart.

Board Games

Four-year-olds love to play board games. Try these favorites.

What You Need

- Checkers®

- Chutes and Ladders®

- Candyland®

- memory games such as Arthur's Memory Game® and the Pooh Memory Game®

What You Do

Follow the directions for the board game you choose.

Hints:

- If your child gets tired of playing, stop.

- Gently suggest strategies.

- Eliminate your "killer" instinct, but don't give up modeling strategies for winning.

- Compliment good moves.

- Enjoy the game!

A Pattern Pole

Count and pattern with cereal.

What You Need

- a glob of clay
- a stir stick or a skewer (cut off pointed end)
- colored loop cereal

What You Do

1. Stand stick upright in the glob of clay to make a pole.

2. Put cereal on the pole, one piece at a time.

3. Count the pieces on the pole.

4. Make a pattern by putting on the colored pieces in a specific order.

   yellow • red • yellow • red • yellow • red

Create a Scrapbook

Use paper from grocery bags to create a special scrapbook.

What You Need

- big brown paper grocery bags
- scissors
- paste
- pictures (cut from a magazine, drawn, or photographs)

- hole punch
- yarn or string
- marking pen

What You Do

Making the Scrapbook

1. Cut bags into three 9" x 12" (23 x 30.5 cm) rectangles.

2. Fold the rectangles in half. Open the rectangles flat.

3. Stack the brown paper rectangles on top of each other.

4. Refold the papers and then punch three holes through the pages. Bind the book by tying yarn through the holes.

Filling the Scrapbook

1. Write your child's name on the cover of the scrapbook.

2. Cut pictures from magazines, draw them, or use photos. Paste the pictures in the book.

3. Label the pictures with simple words. It's best if your child suggests the words and you write them.

Reading the Scrapbook

1. Look through the pictures.

2. Point to the words as you read them.

3. Talk about the pictures in the book.

Make a Pair

Match the socks in the laundry basket.

What You Need

• clean, unmatched socks from laundry

(Use pairs of socks of different colors and sizes as you begin sorting. Don't expect your four-year-old to sort a pile of white athletic socks.)

What You Do

1. Spread the socks out on a large surface. The floor works well.

2. Hold up one sock. Look with your child to find its mate.

3. Repeat until all the socks are matched.

Doing something real puts value in the effort. Make sure that you deliver the socks to their owners with the report that your child helped do the sorting!

indoor playtime • indoor playtime • indoor playtime • indoor playtime • indoor playtime • indoor playtime • indoor playtime • indoor playtime • indoo

Seed Starter

Plant seeds in egg carton cups to observe the beginning stages of plant growth.

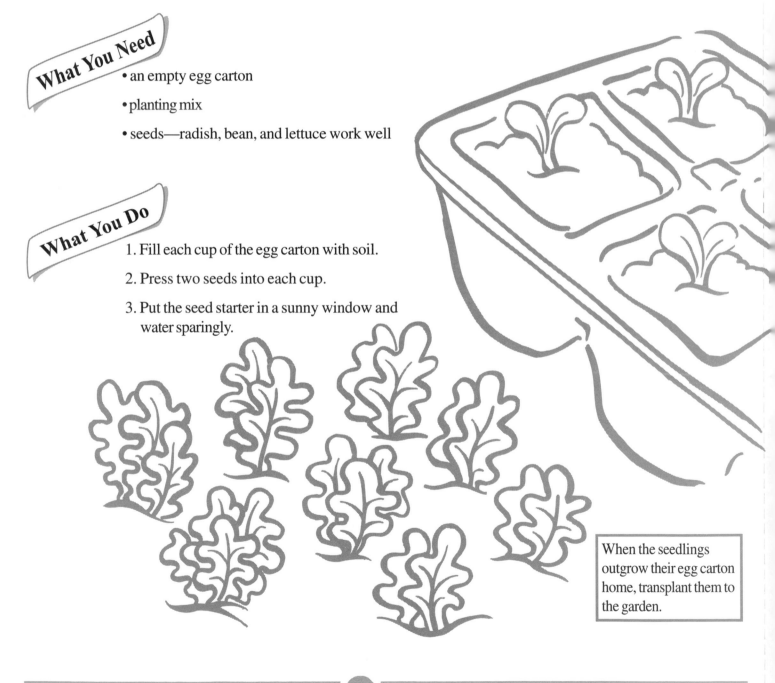

What You Need

- an empty egg carton
- planting mix
- seeds—radish, bean, and lettuce work well

What You Do

1. Fill each cup of the egg carton with soil.

2. Press two seeds into each cup.

3. Put the seed starter in a sunny window and water sparingly.

When the seedlings outgrow their egg carton home, transplant them to the garden.

Play and Learn with Your Four-Year-Old • EMC 4503

Clean-Up Contest

Put things away and collect the household trash.

What You Need

- a room with things to be put away

- a large garbage bag or trash can

What You Do

1. Set a time goal. Say,

   *Let's see if we can collect all the trash
   in 10 minutes.*

   *Let's see if we can put the toys on the
   shelves in 5 minutes.*

2. Work side-by-side with your child to complete
   the job.

   - Hold the large trash bag and let your child empty the small
     trash containers from each room into the bag.

   - Pick up the blocks as your child picks up the books.

3. Check the clock as you finish to see if you accomplished your goal.

Building Towers

Plan and build towers, fences, and block communities.

What You Need

• a set of blocks—purchase a set of wooden or plastic blocks, or make your own from milk cartons

Milk Carton Blocks
Wash empty half-gallon milk cartons.
Open the lips and tear open the top flaps.
Cut down the four corners and fold flat.
Tape the end with clear tape.
Cover the milk carton block with contact paper. (optional)

What You Do

Sit on the floor with your child and begin.

To Build a Tower

1. Take turns stacking blocks.

2. After the tower collapses, change the tower by:
   • placing the foundation blocks in a different position
   • using several blocks for each layer
   • starting with several blocks at the bottom and using fewer blocks on each level

To Build a Fence in a Pattern

1. Line up four blocks using a simple pattern.

2. Have your child copy the pattern to extend the fence.

3. Let your child create the pattern.

4. You extend the fence.

Try more complicated patterns as your child's expertise increases.

Balance It

Challenge your child to find ways to balance a variety of objects.

What You Need

- a beanbag

- a ball

- a book

What You Do

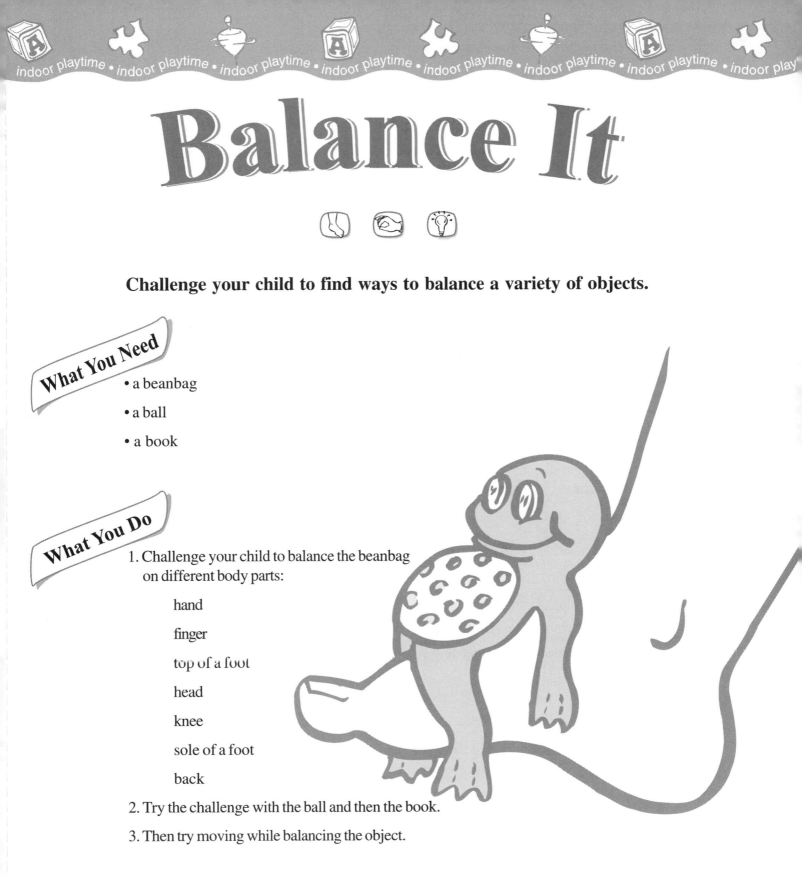

1. Challenge your child to balance the beanbag on different body parts:

   hand

   finger

   top of a foot

   head

   knee

   sole of a foot

   back

2. Try the challenge with the ball and then the book.

3. Then try moving while balancing the object.

A Paper Cup Tower

See how tall you can make your paper cup tower.

What You Need

- paper cups
- cardboard or posterboard dividers (any size will do)
- a flat surface

What You Do

1. Put three cups upside down on the flat surface.
2. Lay a piece of cardboard on top of the cups.
3. Put three more cups on top of the cardboard.
4. Continue alternating cups and cardboard. Say,

    How tall can you make the tower?

    What happens when you change the number of cups? the position of the cups?

    What happens if you change the size of the divider?

    What happens if you put the cups upright?

Domino Snake

Create a domino snake and then enjoy watching it collapse.

What You Need

- a set of dominoes
- a flat surface

What You Do

1. Stand dominoes close together in a row.

2. Tip the first domino over and watch the chain reaction.

See how long you can make the row before the dominoes topple over.

Try making your snake go under a table or chair and out the other side.

Don't Tip the Tray!

Carrying a tray successfully requires an understanding of balance points.

What You Need

- a plastic tray
- blocks, plastic tumblers, other small toys

Note: Do this activity with nonbreakable items.

What You Do

1. Balance the tray on one hand.

2. Have your child pile blocks on one end of the tray. Ask,
   What happened?

3. Challenge your child to think of a way to pile the blocks on the tray so that it doesn't tip over.

4. Have your child balance the tray and tell you where to pile the blocks.

After you and your child have explored the idea of balancing, serve a snack on the tray.

Outdoor Playtime

Throwing and catching,
Taking a walk,
Planning a picnic,
Pausing to talk.
Playing outdoors
Is good for me.
It helps me learn
And it is free.

Play and Learn to

- run, jump, hop, skip, and climb
- throw, catch, kick, and bounce balls
- balance
- identify sounds
- see construction equipment at work
- dig in sand and dirt

Activities

Follow the Leader

March, hop, and skip in this traditional copycat game.

What You Need

- a large open space

What You Do

1. Decide who will be the leader.

2. The leader leads the way. Skip or run or walk or tiptoe around the open space.

3. The follower follows, imitating the leader's movements.

4. Change leaders after a few minutes.

Vary the game:

- add arm movements
- maneuver around trees or play equipment
- invite others to join your fun

Play and Learn with Your Four-Year-Old • EMC 4503

Water Painting

"Paint" walls, trees, fences, gates, mailboxes, and lawn furniture with water.

What You Need

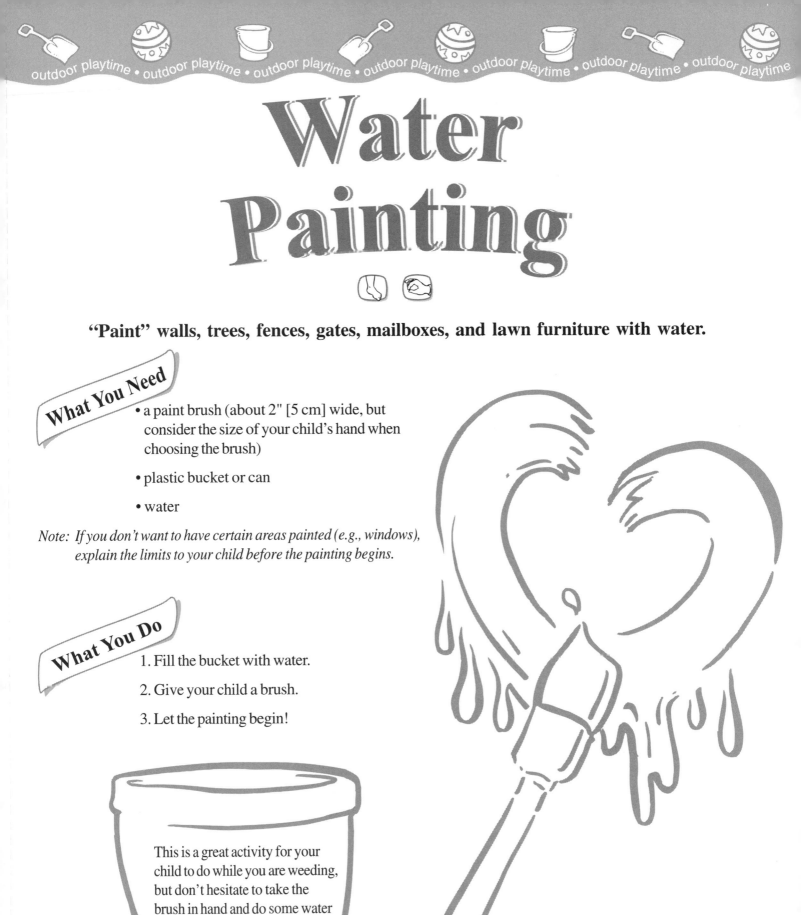

- a paint brush (about 2" [5 cm] wide, but consider the size of your child's hand when choosing the brush)

- plastic bucket or can

- water

Note: If you don't want to have certain areas painted (e.g., windows), explain the limits to your child before the painting begins.

What You Do

1. Fill the bucket with water.

2. Give your child a brush.

3. Let the painting begin!

This is a great activity for your child to do while you are weeding, but don't hesitate to take the brush in hand and do some water painting yourself.

Catch and Kick

Practice throwing, catching, and kicking.

What You Need

• balls of varying sizes—
foam balls for beginning throwing and catching
beach balls
playground balls or soccer balls for kicking

What You Do

Throwing and Catching

1. Stand about 5 feet from your child. Throw the foam ball.

2. Your child catches the ball and throws it back.

Enjoy the play as you model correct throwing and catching.
Be supportive.
    Good catch. Nice try.
Use different balls as your child becomes proficient.

Kicking

1. Roll the ball to your child. Your child kicks the ball.

2. You catch the ball and roll it again.

Switch places occasionally, but keep your kicks under
control. You might want to enlist several others to join
in the kicking fun. Keep it simple and noncompetitive.

Happy Day Hopscotch

Play this variation of traditional hopscotch.

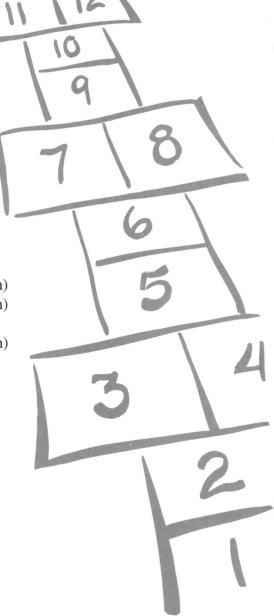

What You Need

- a hard surface
- chalk or stick for marking the hopscotch pattern

What You Do

1. Draw the pattern shown on the playing surface. (Scratch the pattern with a stick if you're playing on dirt or sand.)

2. Start at square number one and hop, chanting the rhyme as you go. On side-by-side squares use both feet.

   Hop, Hop, Hopscotch,   (hop, hop, both feet down)
   Hop, Hop, Hopscotch,   (hop, hop, both feet down)
   Happy Day, Happy Day,
   Hopscotch!   (hop, hop, both feet down)

3. Take turns hopping through the pattern. Vary the game by:
   - telling something that makes your day happy as you complete the jumping
   - repeating the verse and jumping back through the pattern. Repeat the last "hopscotch" twice and do a turn before you start back.

Scoop and Throw

Develop eye-hand coordination with this throwing and catching game.

What You Need

- a beanbag
- two one-gallon plastic containers with handles

Making the Scoops
Use clean one-gallon plastic containers to make the scoops. Cut the containers as shown.

What You Do

1. Stand about four feet from your child.

2. One of you will put the beanbag in one scoop and move the scoop forward to throw the bag.

3. The other one will catch the beanbag in his or her scoop.

4. Repeat.

Tightrope Walker

Walk and balance on lines, curbs, and low walls.

What You Need

- chalk or a stick
- a curb
- a low wall

What You Do

1. Draw or scratch a line on the surface.

2. Walk carefully, one foot in front of the other, along the line. Extend your arms for balance.

3. Repeat until you can walk the line quickly and efficiently.

4. Move to a curb away from a street.

5. Move to a low wall. (Act as a "spotter" as your child walks along this new "tightrope.")

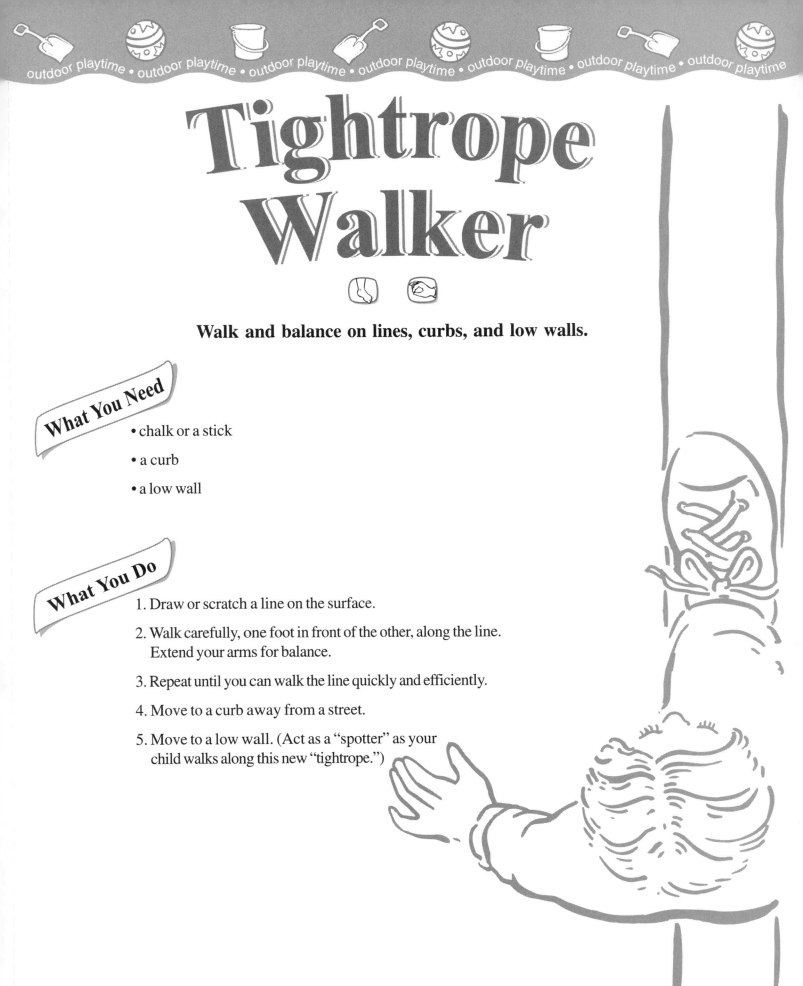

Listening Walk

Walk around your neighborhood focusing on sounds.

What You Need

- a place to walk
- backpack with snack and water bottle (optional)

What You Do

1. Put on comfortable shoes, stick a snack in your backpack, and fill your water bottle.

2. Walk with your child. Listen for the sounds around you as you walk.

3. Talk about the things you see that make the sounds.

4. Take the same walk at a different time of day. Ask,
   Are the sounds the same?
   How are they different?
   Why?

Visit a Construction Site

Watch the giant machinery used to build houses, roads, and buildings.

What You Need

- a construction site
- a camera (optional)

What You Do

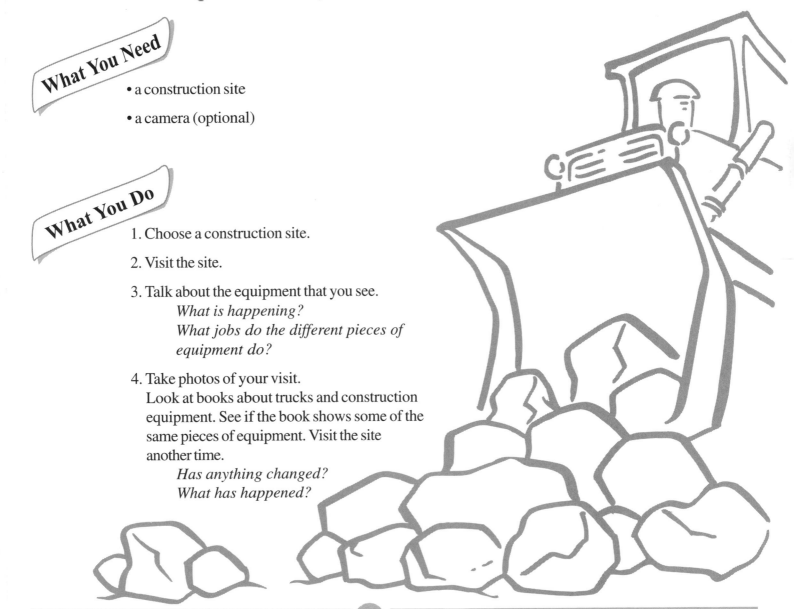

1. Choose a construction site.

2. Visit the site.

3. Talk about the equipment that you see.
   What is happening?
   What jobs do the different pieces of equipment do?

4. Take photos of your visit.
   Look at books about trucks and construction equipment. See if the book shows some of the same pieces of equipment. Visit the site another time.
   Has anything changed?
   What has happened?

Digging

Digging is an adventure. Imagine what you might find!

What You Need

- child-sized shovel or garden trowel
- a place to dig

What You Do

1. Choose a place to dig. Make sure that the sand or dirt in your first location is soft to ensure initial success.

2. Dig!

At first, there is no need for a plan or a strategy. Your child will simply enjoy the accomplishment of digging a hole. As you repeat the experience, ask your child what he or she is digging.

Add water to the experience and you can dig a river. Soon you will be creating and digging interconnecting systems of waterways!

Pack a Picnic

Enjoy the freedom of a picnic.

What You Need

- a container to carry your food
- food
- water
- something to sit on (optional)

What You Do

1. The preparations for a picnic are almost as much fun as the picnic itself and are great opportunities for learning. Give your child responsibility for part of the pre-picnic preparations.
   (Use a recipe from pages 48 or 20.)

2. Let your child help in transporting the food and equipment to the picnic.

3. Spread out the feast and enjoy.

four-year-old picnic favorites

Lettuce Wraps
1. Spread cream cheese on a lettuce leaf.
2. Sprinkle with sunflower seeds.
3. Roll up the leaf.
4. Eat.

Count-it Bags
1. Put in a bag:
   10 Cheerios®
   10 M&M's®
   10 pretzels
   10 peanuts
2. Shake and eat.

Dip-it Fruit
1. Stab a bite-sized piece of fruit with a toothpick.
2. Dip the fruit into yogurt.
3. Eat.

P.B.+ Sandwiches
1. Spread bread with peanut butter.
2. Crumble a piece of bacon over p.b.
3. Dribble honey on top.
4. Add another slice of bread.
5. Nibble.

Vehicle Wash

Set up a station for washing vehicles.

What You Need

- a hose
- a bucket
- a big sponge
- some vehicles—toys, trikes and bikes, or your car!
- a nozzle that has a squeeze off and on (optional)
- markers and cardboard for a sign

What You Do

1. Set up the washing station.

    - Coil the hose with nozzle attached.
    - Set out the bucket and sponge.
    - Make a sign—*Tommy's Wash and Shine*

2. Start washing.

The same kind of washing station is a great way to clean toys and play dishes.

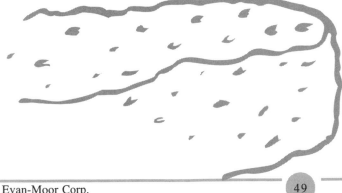

Bedtime

Please tuck me in.
It's our special time.
We'll end the day
With a goodnight rhyme.

Play and Learn to

- memorize rhymes
- practice fingerplays
- tell stories
- listen and remember
- make comparisons
- discover how light moves
- talk about before and after

Activities

Fingerplays

Chant and sing simple rhyming verses as you do hand and finger actions.

What You Need

- a rhyme in your head (see page 52)

What You Do

When you first introduce a fingerplay, do it for your child several times. Sit on the bed facing your child and enjoy the fun. Suggest that your child join in and imitate your actions if he or she does not do so automatically.

Learn the fingerplays on the next page one at a time. Then establish a bedtime fingerplay routine as you repeat both of them each night.

Substitute a new rhyme when you find one that's fun. Remember, bedtime is a quiet time so the fingerplays that you are looking for at this point can include giggling and fun, but should not overstimulate your child.

Fingerplays for Four-Year-Olds

Open, Shut Them

Open, shut them.
Open, shut them.
Give a little clap.

Open, shut them.
Open, shut them.
Put them in your lap.

Creep them, creep them.
Creep them, creep them
Right up to your chin.

Open wide your little mouth
But do not let them in.

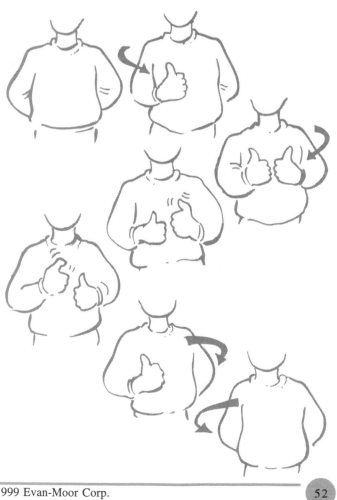

Where Is Thumbkin?

Where is Thumbkin?
Where is Thumbkin?
Here I am. Here I am.
How are you tonight, sir?
Very well, I thank you.
Run away.
Run away.
(Repeat with Pointer, Tall Man,
Ring Man, Pinky)

Before and After

Talk about what comes before and what comes after.

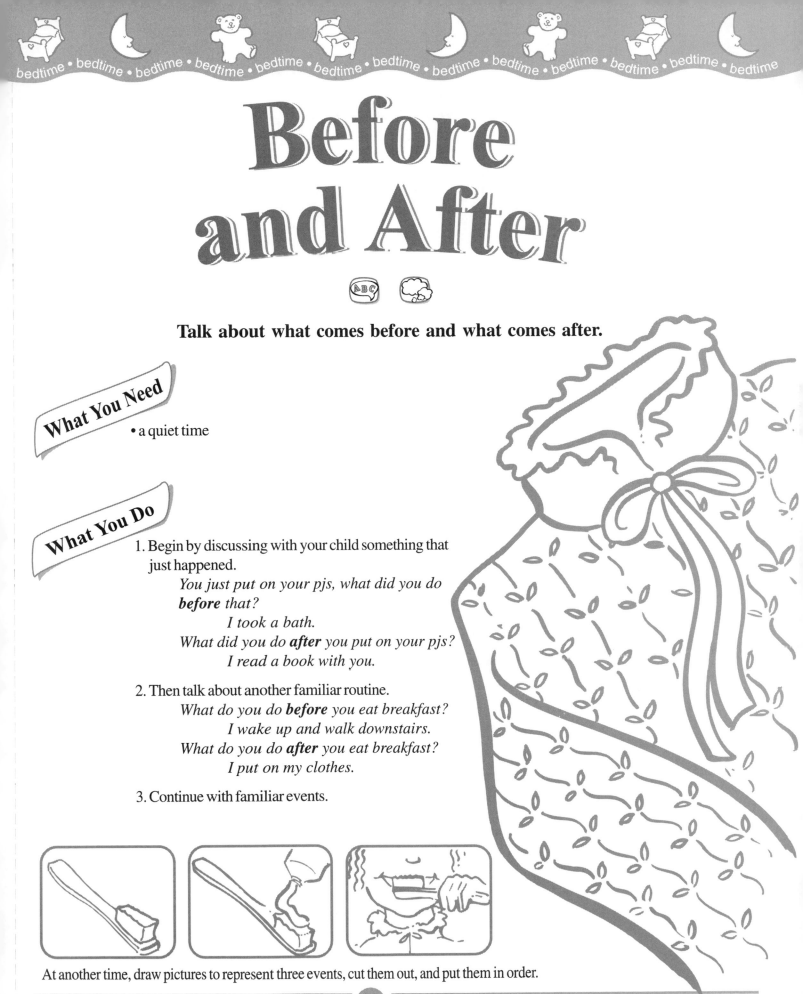

What You Need

• a quiet time

What You Do

1. Begin by discussing with your child something that just happened.

   You just put on your pjs, what did you do **before** *that?*
   > *I took a bath.*

   What did you do **after** *you put on your pjs?*
   > *I read a book with you.*

2. Then talk about another familiar routine.

   What do you do **before** *you eat breakfast?*
   > *I wake up and walk downstairs.*

   What do you do **after** *you eat breakfast?*
   > *I put on my clothes.*

3. Continue with familiar events.

At another time, draw pictures to represent three events, cut them out, and put them in order.

Decorate a Pillowcase

Do this drawing activity anytime. Talk about your pictures at bedtime.

What You Need

- prewashed white pillowcase
- fabric crayons (Buy them at a craft store or a fabric store.)
- drawing paper
- a piece of cardboard
- iron

What You Do

1. Draw a picture on a piece of paper.

2. Put a piece of cardboard inside the pillowcase to keep the color from going through.

3. Put the picture crayon-side down on the pillowcase.

4. Hold a hot iron on the drawing.

5. Lift the iron and remove the paper. The drawing will be transferred to the pillowcase.

6. Use marking pens to add messages or captions.

Note: The picture may be reused by going over the outline again with the fabric crayons.

Invent a Story

Take turns telling parts of a story.

What You Need

• imagination

What You Do

1. Start a story.
   Parent: *There was once a little girl named Amy. She had a new kitten. She was trying to think of a name for the kitten.*

2. Have your child continue.
   Child: *Amy named it Rainbow Patches Peanut Butter.*

3. Continue taking turns to complete the story.
   Parent: *Everyone who came to visit asked Amy what the kitten's name was. Amy always said, "Rainbow Patches Peanut Butter." Then everyone asked, "Why did you name it Rainbow Patches Peanut Butter?"*
   Child: *'Cause that's a good name. So Amy and Rainbow Patches Peanut Butter had many more adventures. The End.*

Hints:

• Stories should be about familiar events at first.

• Keep the stories short.

• Develop characters that are repeated in subsequent stories.

Light and Dark

Turn the lights off and on to compare what you see when it's light and when it's dark.

What You Need

• a light switch

What You Do

1. Turn out the lights and ask,
    What can you see in the dark?

2. Talk about the things that you see.

3. Turn on the lights and repeat.

Another time, look out the window and ask,
    What do you see outside when it's dark?
    When it's light?

My Flashlight

Shine a flashlight at objects in the bedroom to see that light goes where it's pointed.

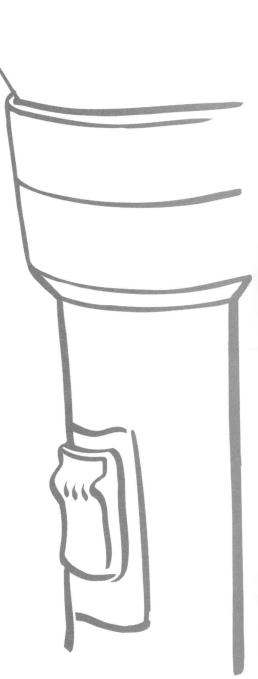

What You Need

- flashlight
- dark room

What You Do

1. Turn the lights off.

2. Point the flashlight at an object across the bedroom.

3. Turn the flashlight on. Ask,
   What do you see?

4. Turn the flashlight off.

5. Point the flashlight at a different object.

6. Turn the flashlight on. Ask,
   What do you see?
   Why did what you see change?

(Your child may say, *The flashlight is pointed at the new thing.*
Or *You moved the light.*)

7. Have your child point and shine the flashlight several times.

Another time:
Block the light by putting your hand or a stuffed animal between
the flashlight and the object. Ask,
   What stopped the light?

While-You-Wait Time

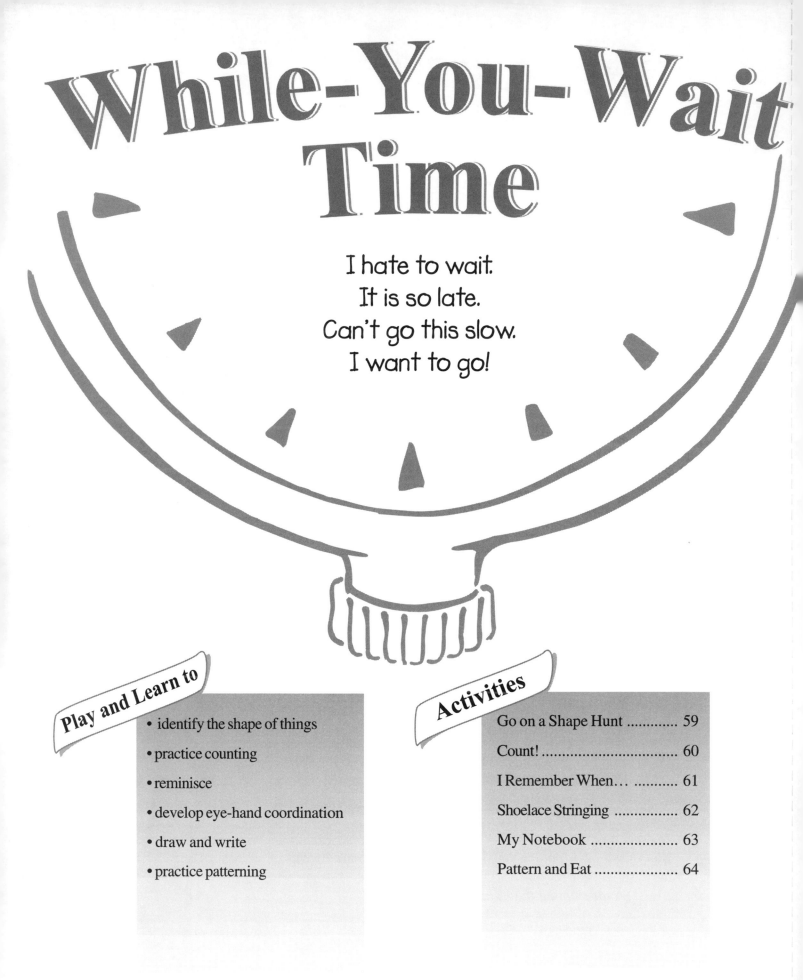

I hate to wait.
It is so late.
Can't go this slow.
I want to go!

Play and Learn to

- identify the shape of things
- practice counting
- reminisce
- develop eye-hand coordination
- draw and write
- practice patterning

Activities

Go on a Shape Hunt

Name all of the things around you that have a specific shape.

What You Need

• the things around you

What You Do

1. Think of a shape. Say,
   a square

2. Look around and name all the things that are that shape.
   the window, the book, the table, the sign

3. Change shapes.

4. Find combinations of shapes. Say,
   Can you find something that is a circle and a square?

Count!

Practice counting.

What You Need

• nothing!

What You Do

Just count! Count together in different ways.

• Partner Count
  You say one number.
  Your child says the next number.

• All by Myself
  Your child counts and you listen.

• Count Big Numbers
  101, 102, 103, 104, 105, ...

• Count Backwards
  10, 9, 8, 7, ...

• Count by Tens
  10, 20, 30, 40, ...

• Count by Fives
  5, 10, 15, 20, ...

while-you-wait time • while-you-wait time • while-you-wait time • while-you-wait time • while-you-wait time • while-you-wait time

I Remember When...

Reminisce about events in your child's past.

What You Need

• memories

What You Do

1. Recall an event and tell about it.

   I remember when you were two and you wore a jack-o-lantern costume for the Halloween parade. The pumpkin's smile had two teeth. Daddy even stuffed the costume with diapers to make you look rounder.

2. Your child will love hearing your memories and will often ask for more details.

   Did you carry me or did I walk?

Soon your child will fill waiting time with his or her own memories.

Shoelace Stringing

Stuck at a meeting or an appointment without a toy? Use a shoe!

What You Need

• a shoe with shoestrings

What You Do

1. Take the shoestring out of a shoe.

2. Restring the string. You may need to demonstrate how to do this and help with the initial steps. Remember, your goal is fun and practice in eye-hand coordination. Don't expect perfectly laced shoes. Laugh together over problems.

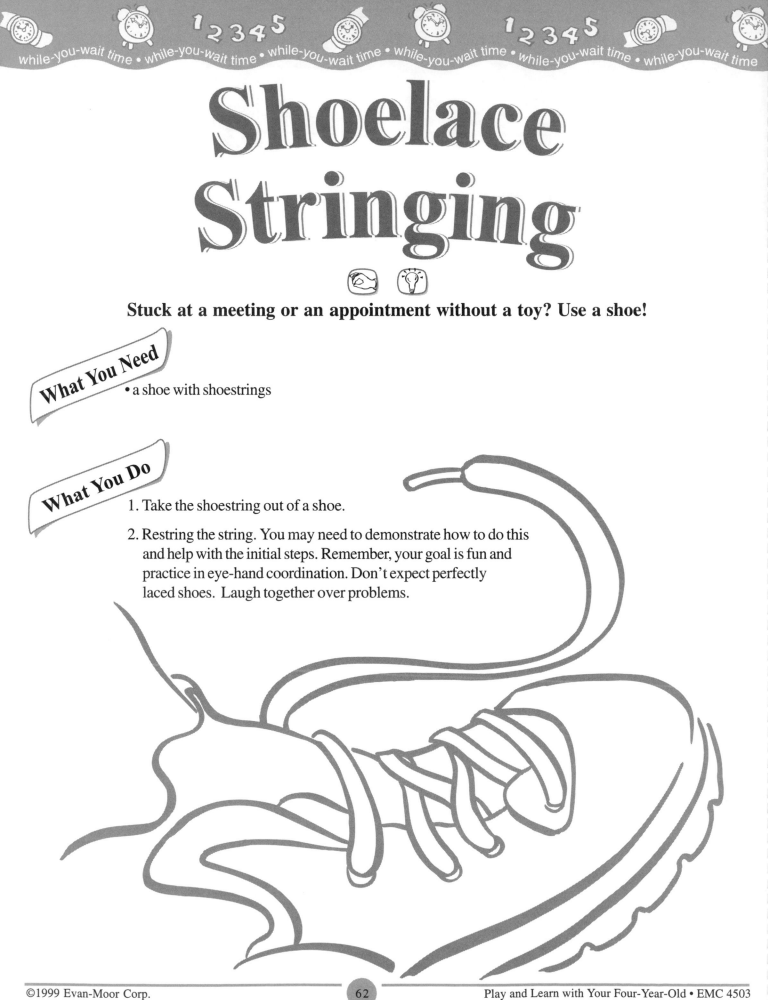

My Notebook

For creating while waiting, carry a small notebook with pencil.

What You Need

- a small notebook—a memo-sized spiral one is great
- a pencil
- a string

What You Do

1. Attach the pencil to the notebook. Tie the string to the spiral or punch a hole in the cover.

2. Keep the notebook in your purse or pocket so it's always handy.

Try these animals:

Dog

Cat

Mouse

Elephant

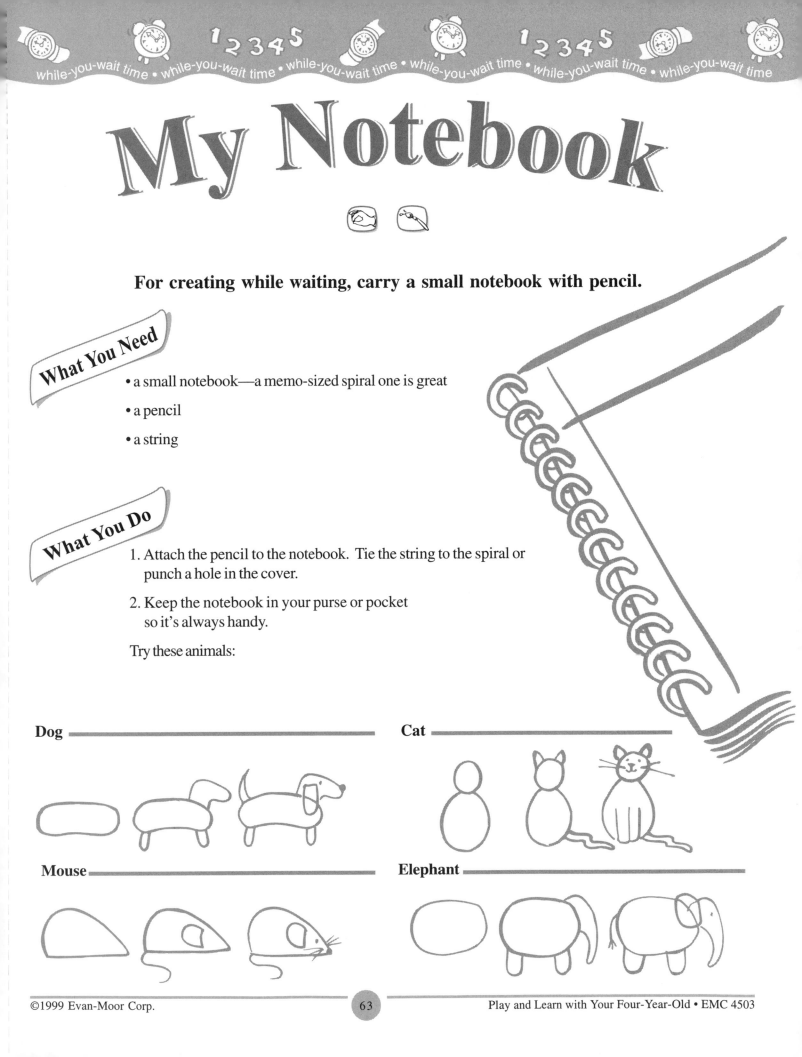

Pattern and Eat

Carry a plastic container of small snacks for patterning fun.

What You Need

• small plastic container with lid

• little nibbles like Cheerios®, raisins, grapes, marshmallows, ...

• a piece of paper

What You Do

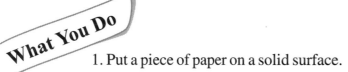

1. Put a piece of paper on a solid surface.

2. Put a patterned line of 4–6 nibbles at the top of the paper.
    grape • grape • marshmallow • marshmallow • grape • grape

3. Have your child duplicate the line.

4. Eat the pattern.

Make more complicated patterns.

Play and Learn with Your Four-Year-Old • EMC 4503

Travel Time

We're on the go
Now I must know.
        Are we there yet?
It's been so long
Let's sing a song.
        Are we there yet?
I'm feeling sick.
Stop really quick.
        Are we there yet?
How 'bout a snack
Out of your sack?
        Are we there yet?
I see Grandpa.
I see Grandma.
        We're there!

Play and Learn to

- count
- name things
- identify colors
- recite rhymes
- imagine
- pattern
- record information
- tell stories

Activities

The Passing Game

Tally the vehicles that go by.

What You Need

• paper on clipboard

• crayon

What You Do

1. Divide your sheet of paper in half.

2. Decide on two vehicles to watch for. Label the two sides of the tally sheet.

3. Put a mark on the record sheet to count each vehicle as you spy it.

Add another category.

Note: If you're traveling on a busy freeway, designate specific cars or trucks to tally—tow trucks and blue vans. If you're traveling on a country road, make the categories more general—pickups and cars.

Books & Songs on Tape

Sing along with a tape or turn the pages as you listen to your favorite book on tape.

What You Need

- an audiotape
- a tape player

What You Do

Listen!

Use headphones or rear-seat speakers on long trips when the same song or story becomes tiresome to you.

travel time • travel time • travel time • travel time • travel time • travel time • travel time • travel time • travel time • travel time • travel t

Traffic Light Verse

Model good driving for your four-year-old.

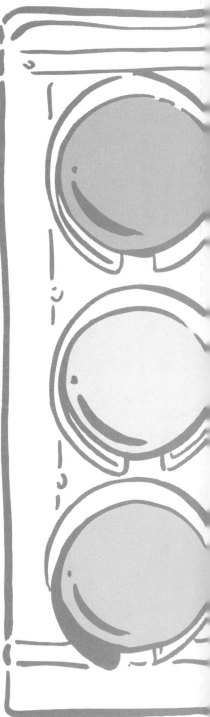

What You Need

- a traffic light situation

What You Do

1. Explain what the colors on a traffic light mean by teaching this verse or your own version of it.

   Red light means STOP.
   Green light means GO.
   Yellow means look before you know
   Whether to stop or whether to go.

2. As you approach a traffic light repeat the appropriate line. Say, *(color) light,* and have your child finish the line.

S-T-O-P Spells Stop

Teach your child to recognize a stop sign.

• a stop sign

What You Do

1. Point out a stop sign as you drive or as you walk.

2. Note the color and the shape.

3. Ask,
   What does it say?
   (Your child probably knows that it says STOP, if not, explain that it does.)

4. Point to the letters and say, *S - T - O - P spells Stop.*

5. Repeat the words whenever you pass a stop sign.

When you want your child to stop doing something, try spelling *S-T-O-P.*

Colorforms® on the Window

Colorforms® provide entertainment for long road trips.

What You Need

• flexible plastic paper shapes and figures

Make your own color shapes from Rubbermaid® shelf-liner paper or purchase ready-made shapes (Colorforms®) from a toy store.

What You Do

1. Put the color shapes on the car window:
   • Make a picture.

   • Arrange the shapes in groups with similar attributes.

   • Count how many you have.

   • Make a line of shapes across the window.

   • Make a line of shapes from the top to the bottom of the window.

2. Tell about the color shapes:
   • Talk about the picture.

   • Ask about the "rules" used for making the groups.

   • Count the shapes together.

Drawing Tray

Keep a travel tray in the car for long and short trips.

What You Need

- a plastic tray with a smooth surface
- zippered pouch or zip-lock plastic bag
- paper
- crayons
- Colorforms® shapes
- pencil

What You Do

1. Put the objects in the pouch.

2. Put the tray in the car so you're ready whenever you're on the go.

Pipe Cleaners and Cheerios®

String Cheerios® on a pipe cleaner.

What You Need

- pipe cleaners
- container of Cheerios®

What You Do

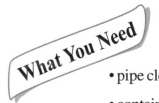

1. Bend one end of a pipe cleaner up as shown.

2. String Cheerios® onto the straight end of the pipe cleaner.

3. Bend the other end up when stringing is completed.

4. Unbend to nibble the treats!

After your child has done the activity several times, vary the task:

- Count the Cheerios® you used.

- Put 10 Cheerios® on the pipe cleaner.

- Use Fruit Loops® and create a pattern.
  red • red • orange • orange • red • red •

Story Time

I love to tell stories and read them, too.
We can act them out. It's fun to do!
Let's use puppets. Let's make a rhyme.
We have great fun at story time.

Play and Learn to

- build a sense of extended family

- tell and retell stories

- predict what will happen next

- identify objects in illustrations and photographs

- act out stories

- make and use puppets

- turn pages, start from the front of a book, and understand that a word stands for the name of a thing

Activities

Shared Reading

Sit your child on your lap or snuggle together on the bed and share a favorite book.

What You Need

• a good book

What You Do

1. Read with feeling.

2. Let your child participate by:
    filling in words
    turning pages
    pointing out pictures
    talking about the story

A few suggestions:

Bookstores and libraries are filled with wonderful books for you and your child to share. There are a number of excellent read-aloud guides that will help you choose good literature appropriate for the age of your child.

Buy a few special books to enjoy over and over again at bedtime. Be sure to consider the following categories:

• Beautiful picture books like
    The Mare on the Hill by Thomas Locker; Dial Books, 1985.
• Books with flaps or hidden pictures like
    Eric Hill's *Spot* books
• Books with wonderful sounds and great rhyme like
    Dr. Seuss's *ABC Book* and *Hop on Pop*

• Books with appealing stories
    The Best Nest by P.D. Eastman; Random House Beginner Books, 1968.
    Cookie's Week by Cindy Ward; Scholastic, 1988.

This is my teddy He has a crown and I love him.

• Nonfiction books

Richard Scarry's *Cars and Trucks and Things That Go;* Western Publishing Company, 1974.

• Lullabies

Hush Little Baby by Sylvia Long; Chronicle Books, 1997.

• Books on topics 4-year-olds can relate to

All By Myself by Mercer Mayer; Western Publishing Company, 1983.

Practice important prereading skills as you read.

> Don't do this with every story.
> Don't do all the things at once.
> Do enjoy reading.
> Do practice these prereading strategies often.

1. Retelling

Your child's ability to retell, to summarize, and to order the events in a story are indicators of reading readiness. When you have finished reading a story, ask your child to tell what the story was about.

Tell me about what happened in the story.

2. Predicting

Stop reading and ask your child to predict what will happen next. Listen carefully and then read on to see if the prediction was correct.

3. Identifying Pictures

Point to a picture. Say,

Tell me what this is.

or

Show me a _____.

And have your child point to an object.

Family Stories and Photos

Enjoy true stories about family members

What You Need

- photos of family members
- stories

What You Do

1. Identify a photo.
   This is Grandma Jill.

2. Tell the story.
   My son tells his children this true story about me when I was a child. I used to tell it to him.

   When Grandma was a little girl she had a horse named Charlie. She loved to ride Charlie in the pasture. One day Grandma Jill had a friend over to play and they decided to ride Charlie. Charlie enjoyed the attention until the two girls took him out into the big wheat field. He saw something that scared him and jumped to the side. Both Grandma and her friend fell off and Charlie ran home. It was a sad day because both girls broke their arms when they fell. They never found out what made Charlie jump.

   Keep a photo gallery of special family members on the refrigerator. Refer to it as you tell family stories.

Act It Out

Enjoy dramatic play as you retell your favorite stories.

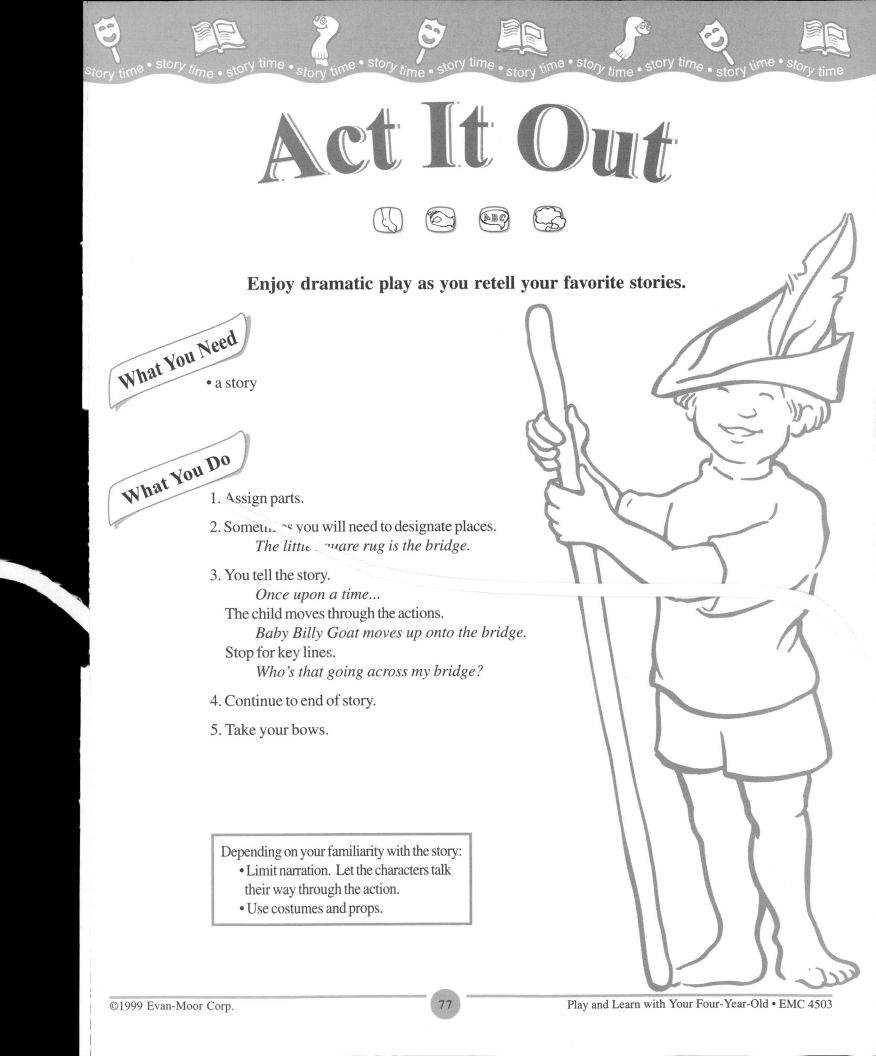

What You Need

- a story

What You Do

1. Assign parts.

2. Someti... ... you will need to designate places.
   The littl... ...uare rug is the bridge.

3. You tell the story.
   Once upon a time...
   The child moves through the actions.
   Baby Billy Goat moves up onto the bridge.
   Stop for key lines.
   Who's that going across my bridge?

4. Continue to end of story.

5. Take your bows.

Depending on your familiarity with the story:
- Limit narration. Let the characters talk their way through the action.
- Use costumes and props.

Puppets

Four-year-olds love puppets. Use them to retell old stories, make up new stories, or just talk.

What You Need

- puppets—buy ready-made ones or make your own (see page 79)

What You Do

1. Put a puppet on your hand.

2. Give one to your child.

3. Start talking as the puppet.
   Begin with a familiar story like *The Gingerbread Man*.
   Try a familiar situation like going to bed.
   Try out a new situation like visiting Grandma alone.

Paper Bag Puppet Directions

Materials:

- small brown paper lunch bag
- marking pens or crayons

Steps:

1. Draw faces on flap of bag. The bottom of the flap is the top of the puppet's mouth.

2. Draw or decorate the rest of the bag.

To use the puppet: Put hand inside bag with fingers extending into the flap. Move fingers up and down to make mouth move.

Finger Puppet Directions

Materials:

- finger
- washable marking pen
- small piece of yarn

Steps:

1. Draw a face on a finger.

2. Tie a yarn necktie on the finger.

To use the puppet: Move your finger and talk.

A Collection of Stories

Record your child's stories and add pictures to create a special collection.

What You Need

- a computer or traditional writing tools
- paper
- photos or child-drawn illustrations
- a scrapbook

What You Do

1. Write a story down as your child tells it.

2. Take photos or draw pictures to illustrate the story.

3. Mount the story and illustrations on scrapbook pages.

4. Read and enjoy.

Note the date the story was written and any other interesting circumstances. The scrapbook will become an important keepsake.

We went to Farm Day at the Fairgrounds. We saw turkeys.